CHEETAHS

EYE TO EYE WITH BIG CATS

Jason Cooper

Rourke

www.rourkepublishing.com

PHOTO CREDITS: Page 17 © JoeMcDonald/Animals Animals; all other photos © Lynn M. Stone.

Cover Photo: *Cheetahs live on the grassy plains of Africa, where they use their great speed to chase down hoofed prey.*

Editor: Frank Sloan

Cover design by Nicola Stratford

Library of Congress Cataloging-in-Publication Data

Cooper, Jason, 1942-
  Cheetahs / Jason Cooper.
     v. cm. – (Eye to eye with big cats)
Includes bibliographical references (p.   ).
Contents: The cheetah — The cheetah's relatives — What cheetahs look like — Where cheetahs live — How cheetahs live — The cheetah's cubs — Predators and prey — Cheetahs and people.
  ISBN 1-58952-401-2 (hardcover)
  1. Cheetah--Juvenile literature. [1. Cheetah. 2. Endangered species.]
I. Title.

  QL737.C23 C674 2002
  599.75'9—dc21

                                                      2002003571

Printed in the USA

CG/CG

TABLE OF CONTENTS

The Cheetah   5
The Cheetah's Relatives   6
What Cheetahs Look Like   9
Where Cheetahs Live   11
How Cheetahs Live   14
Cheetah Cubs   16
Predator and Prey   19
Cheetahs and People   20
The Future of Cheetahs   22
Glossary   23
Index   24
Further Reading/Websites to Visit   24

THE CHEETAH

The cheetah *(Acinonyx jubatus)* is a big, spotted cat. It is actually the fastest mammal known. It can run for bursts of speed that reach 70 miles (112 kilometers) an hour. Because of its speed, the cheetah's feet are off the ground for half the distance it races.

A cheetah runs at these speeds to catch its **prey**. But the creature can only run at top speed for short distances. If it doesn't catch the animal, the cheetah has to stop to rest.

An alert cheetah, looking for prey

THE CHEETAH'S RELATIVES

Cheetahs are related to all the cats, known as **felines.** But they are unlike most of the cat family. Cheetah claws are not hidden, nor are they sharply curved. The pads on their feet are short and tough. Their legs and paws are slim.

There are as many as eight different types of cheetahs. They are all closely related.

A cheetah's claws are exposed. The pads on its feet are more like a dog's.

WHAT CHEETAHS LOOK LIKE

Male cheetahs weigh about 125 pounds (56 kilograms). Cheetahs are taller and slimmer than leopards. They have small heads.

Cheetahs have yellow fur with black spots. They have deep-set eyes and black stripes from their eye corners to their mouths. Cheetahs have deep chests that hold large lungs and a strong heart. These help the cheetah achieve great speed.

A cheetah has stripes that lead from its eyes to the mouth.

WHERE CHEETAHS LIVE

The cheetah lives in several countries of Africa. But it is probably **extinct** outside of Africa. This means that cheetahs in Asia have most likely disappeared.

The cheetah likes to live in open spaces. This is known as its **habitat**. Cheetahs like grassland, plains, and brush country. They do not like trees, because trees keep down the cheetah's speed.

A cheetah walks across a grassy plain in Africa.

A topi antelope watches as cheetahs hunt smaller game.

The cheetah's meal leaves blood on its face.

HOW CHEETAHS LIVE

Most big cats like to rest. But cheetahs like to hunt every few days. Cheetahs need to eat their kill quickly. They are too slender to defend their food against lions, wild dogs, hyenas, and leopards.

Cheetahs spend some time in groups, and males even hunt together.

A cheetah on the run

CHEETAH CUBS

A cheetah's litter often has four cubs. They are born blind and are gray, without spots. The mother raises them on her milk and on meat from kills. At three months, the cubs no longer depend on milk. Their spots begin to appear.

The cubs learn how to hunt. They will leave their mother when they are about a year and half old.

By the time they are a year old, cheetahs kill some of their own prey.

PREDATOR AND PREY

Cheetahs can be playful. But they are **predators**, or hunters. They have excellent sight. Cheetahs run after their prey. They knock the animal down and grab it by the throat.

Cheetahs kill many different animals. Because they are not strong, cheetahs eat their prey where they kill it. Cheetah cubs can even be prey for larger cats.

Cheetahs stop to catch their breath after killing a young wildebeest.

19

CHEETAHS AND PEOPLE

For years, people tamed and trained cheetahs to hunt for them. The use of cheetahs as trained hunters is called **coursing**. This practice may have begun 5,000 years ago. Most cheetahs are not dangerous to humans.

African national parks help keep cheetahs safe from poachers.

THE FUTURE OF CHEETAHS

In Africa the cheetah's habitat is being turned into farmland. This means the cheetah is threatened. Farmers also kill cheetahs. The animals' spotted coat is valuable.

Cheetahs need **preserves**, where they can live safely. Without this protection the 10,000 to 15,000 African cheetahs may die out. They may become extinct.

GLOSSARY

coursing (KOR sing) — using hunting animals to chase other animals

extinct (eks TINKT) — no longer existing

felines (FEE linez) — any of the cats

habitat (HAB uh tat) — the area in which an animal lives

predators (PRED uh turz) — animals that kill other animals for food

preserves (pree ZERVZ) — areas where wild animals are protected from humans

prey (PRAY) — an animal that is hunted for food by another animal

INDEX

Africa   11, 22
Asia   11
cheetah cubs   16
coursing   20
extinct   11, 22

habitat   11
leopards   9
predators   19
preserves   22
prey   5, 19

Further Reading

Lantier-Sampon, Patricia. *The Wonder of Cheetahs*. Gareth Stevens, 2001
MacPherson, Winnie. *Cheetahs: Cheetah Magic for Kids*. Gareth Stevens, 2000

Websites To Visit

http://www.awf.org/wildlives/65
http://www.pbs.org/wnet/nature/cheetahs/resc.html
http://www.hlla.com/reference/anafr-cheetahs.html

About The Author

Jason Cooper has written several children's books about a variety of topics for Rourke Publishing, including recent series *China Discovery* and *American Landmarks.* Cooper travels widely to gather information for his books. Two of his favorite travel destinations are Alaska and the Far East.